WALKING WITH A VIRTUOUS WOMAN

JOURNAL & NOTEBOOK

WHITNEY CHILTON

I dedicate this book to my perfect example of a Virtuous Woman. My mother my angel

Rhonda K. Flourney.

May you continue to rest.

Whitney Chilton

ISBN:

9781675256602

Table of Contents

Table of Contents

Click.

Scroll.

"She's pretty."

"Relationship goals."

Scroll.

"Her body is amazing."

"I want her house."

Scroll.

"I wish I had her life."

"I want to switch places with her."

Scroll.

"How did she get so lucky?"

This is the type of conversation some women all over the world have with themselves on a daily basis. It has become much too easy for us to gain access to the intimate parts of other people's lives, through the lens of social media. We often find ourselves desiring what another person has, and even comparing our own lives to theirs. Even if you are not heavily involved in the social media frenzy, it doesn't mean your mind isn't bombarded with images of how a woman should be. They often tell us how we should walk, talk, look, act, and dress. Many have yielded to the world's interpretation of what a woman is. When you don't measure up to the standard, it causes insecurity and low self-esteem to take residence in your life.

The question we must often ask ourselves is, who's influencing me? Who is inspiring me? Whose example am I following? The reasoning behind some of our behavior, can be found in the answer to those questions. As a God-Fearing woman, we must make sure that our influence comes from the word of God. There is absolutely nothing wrong with having someone that you look up to, who can give you words of wisdom, help you make a sound decision, and inspires you. The mentor/ mentee relationship is important in the life of every human being and is also discussed in scripture. Titus 2 encourages the older women to not only live honorably, but also teach the younger women to do the same. Who and what influences us plays a big role in the way that we live.

As you open this book, we are going to gain influence from the Virtuous Woman. She is a woman who is described in detail in Proverbs 31. While walking with her, we will take a detailed look into her life. Our purpose in this task is to grow as Godly Women. We want to make sure that the life that we are living is not only pleasing in the eyes of God; but inspiring to other women. Woman of God, you carry a big charge! There are women who will watch you survive some of life's toughest moments; and be motivated to press through their own struggles. We must walk, live, and love, in a way that encourages women in our reach to live a life that honors God.

Worker

Proverbs 31:13-
"She selects wool and flax and works with eager hands."

Prelude

We live in a society that places a huge emphasis on utilizing every moment to work! Although there's nothing wrong with working, we must be sure that we are working towards a specific purpose. What is your aim? What is your goal? What are you working towards? You don't want to find yourself working with no aim in mind. This is often the reason why people become tired and drained.

They are working tirelessly with no purpose in mind. The virtuous woman 'selects wool and flax.' The word I want you to pay close attention to is selects. She is selective with what she chooses, because she knows what she's working towards. She selects wool and flax because she's creating garments. It wouldn't be smart for her to select grain and barley, because working with those items wouldn't get her the result she's aiming for. As you work, woman of God, with eager hands, make sure the work that you're putting your hands to is instructed by God. I want you to use your time wisely by working smarter, not harder.

As you do what God is instructing you to do, work every assignment with eager hands and with the spirit of excellence. No matter the job, big or small, be honored that God has selected you to do the assignment. You have goals, assignments and responsibilities that will only be accomplished by working with eager hands. To be chosen to do God's work is an honor. Treat it as such.

Prayer Day One:

Lord thank you for every assignment and task that you have placed before me. Thank you for selecting me for the task. Thank you for blessing me with the opportunity to be a worker in your kingdom. Lord, my heart's desire is to be a benefit to your kingdom. I'm ready to go to work for you with enthusiasm and passion. Wherever you place me Lord, I will work. I know that my work for you isn't only about what I do in the church. Teach me Lord to do every assignment that you have given me with excellence. No longer will I do a mediocre job in your name. I declare that I will put my best foot forward in every assignment that you give me. The work that I do, I will do in your name, and I will do it well. For your word says, 'work as unto the Lord and not unto man.' I want my work to be pleasing to you! Father put my hands to work. I want to always be found operating in the work that you've given me. Your word declares, 'be steadfast, unmovable always abounding in the work of the Lord.' I want to always be found working; working towards my goals, working to fulfill my assignment, working to fulfill your purpose for my life.

Declaration

I declare that I will work with excellence; and everything with my name on it will be quality work.

Journal Prompt
What goals do you have?
What are you doing to accomplish them?

_____

_____

_____

_____

_____

_____

_____

_____

_____

_____

_____

_____

_____

_____

_____

_____

_____

_____

Ambitous

Proverbs 31:14-She is like the merchant ships, bringing her food from afar.

Prelude

How motivated are you? On a scale of 1-10, 10 being extremely motivated, how would you rate yourself? The virtuous woman is an ambitious woman, she's extremely motivated to get the job done. The virtuous woman is a go-getter, fearless, and determined, she is the true definition of a boss! She gets her food from afar. Getting her food from afar means she doesn't make any excuses; how will I get there? How much will this cost? Who will help me carry it? Will it be enough? Will it all be gone before I get there? This woman gets up and does what is required of her to get what she needs, she's ambitious! How many times have you made excuses on why you can't get something done?

A lot of times our excuses are a byproduct of the fear that we are harboring in our hearts. We are often afraid that we will fail again; it won't work, what will people say?, so, we use excuses as a cover-up for our fear. I understand that life happens and it can put a damper on your ambition and stifle your determination and scare you into not trying. Let that be the last time that happens! Never again allow life to rob you of your ambition. Those dreams, those visions, those plans that you have...it's time to go after them...be ambitious.

Prayer Day Two:

Father, thank you for divine order and assignment. Thank you, God, for a passion and desire to chase after you and pursue my purpose with no apologies. God, to be honest, I do experience times when I lack motivation. Sometimes things happen in my life that inhibits my desire to dream big. God, I pray that even during unpleasant and difficult moments, that I don't lose ambition. God ignite a fire in me to go far; to not be afraid of the journey before me. I want to excel in life. Don't allow my ambition to die. Allow my ambition to take me to far places; great places. Lord, I won't take the glory for it. Let no flesh glory in your sight. I will always declare that it is because of you that I succeed. Let my ambition take me to places that will bless my family, people that I don't know, and generations of people that I will never meet. God, bless me with ambition to run after all that you have for me. Let my ambition unlock doors to blessings that I didn't even know were possible. Grant me ambition that is rooted in you, and ignited by the desire to serve you and please you.

Declaration:

I declare that I will dream big and chase after all that God has for me with no excuses.

Journal Prompt
What stops you from dreaming big and why?

_____

_____

_____

_____

_____

_____

_____

_____

_____

_____

_____

_____

_____

_____

_____

_____

_____

_____

_____

Selfless

Proverbs 31:15-She gets up while it is still night; she provides food for her family and portions for her female servants.

Prelude

The highest title a person can carry is the title of 'servant.' A servant is a person that is willing to put the needs of others before themselves. It's easy for us to be served; but it takes a humble spirit to serve others. The virtuous woman gets up while it's still night. She provides food for her family, and for those that work for her. Instead of being asleep like everyone else, she's up in the middle of the night, making sure the needs of those around her are met. She sacrifices her time, sleep, comfort to ensure everyone else isn't in need. Woman of God, there will come times when you will have to put others before yourself. How will you handle it? You can't be a selfish servant who is only concerned about her own needs. As a woman of God, be sensitive to the needs of other people; even if their needs are an inconvenience to you.

Prayer Day Three:

God, I first want to thank you for the most selfless act anyone has done; and that's sending your son Jesus Christ to the cross to die for me. I didn't deserve it, there's nothing that I've done or could ever do to earn it. I am forever grateful. Father, thank you for the sacrifice that you made just to reconcile me back to you. Thank you for the display of love. Thank you for compassion. Thank you for being a God that always puts the welfare of His children first. God, your selfless act is just the example that I needed. Teach me Lord, how to be more selfless. Teach me how to be concerned about the needs of others. Remind me Lord, that it's not always about me. Your word declares that the strong are to bare the infirmities of the weak. God strengthen me, so that I can help my brothers and sisters. Remind me God, that I am here to serve. Just as Jesus, I didn't come to be served; I came to serve. Lord guide me so that I can walk in that truth. Lord, if selfishness be present anywhere in me, show me so that I can turn from it. I desire to be a selfless servant. A woman that recognizes the hurts and cries of others matter. Father, be my support, as I do my best to serve others with excellence.

Declaration:

I declare that I will be more selfless. Remember that it's not always about me.

Journal Prompt

I can be more selfless by...
A time that I was selfless was...

_____

_____

_____

_____

_____

_____

_____

_____

_____

_____

_____

_____

_____

_____

_____

_____

_____

Financially Responsible

Proverbs 31:16-She considers a field and buys it; out of her earnings she plants a vineyard.

WALKING WITH A VIRTUOUS WOMAN

Prelude

Raise your hand wherever you are, if you cringed after reading the title, lol. Financial responsibility is an area that most people overlook. What we often fail to realize is that everything God has given us is a gift; and it's our responsibility to take care of that gift. We must make sure that we are being good stewards of everything that God has placed in our hands. It's very inconsiderate for us to take what God has blessed us with and squander it like it's nothing. You must be more cautious in your spending and more intentional about what you use your money on. The virtuous woman considers a field before she buys it. Do you consider the purchase before you unfold that money, or snatch out that debit card? Do you really need another pair of black shoes? You only have two shoulders; is another shoulder bag necessary? How about you cook at home instead? There are so many leaks in our spending that need to be plugged up! Honor God by taking care of what he's giving you. Sis put that item back. You just purchased the same thing last week.

Prayer Day Four:

Father I honor you and I thank you for everything that you've given me. There have been times, both past and present, when I didn't do a good job with handling what you blessed me with. Lord forgive me. I've wasted money on insignificant things. Lord, I want to be a good steward over the money that you have blessed me with. Teach me Lord, to be wise with my finances. I want to be strategic and prayerful with every purchase. Giving you the first of my earnings, knowing that you honor first fruit! Equip my mind and spirit to handle the blessings that you release to me with wisdom. I don't want to waste what you've given me. Teach me Lord, that I don't have to purchase everything that I see. You said in your word in all thy ways acknowledge you and you would direct my paths. Father, I will acknowledge you first, before making purchases large and small. I want to manage what you've blessed me with, with excellence. Recognizing Lord, that all I have is because of you.

Declaration:

I declare that I will manage my finances well; acknowledging God before making purchases both big and small.

Journal Prompt

Besides bills, where do you spend the most money? What are your
financial goals, and how will you accomplish them?
What could you spend less money on?

_____

_____

_____

_____

_____

_____

_____

_____

_____

_____

_____

_____

_____

_____

_____

_____

_____

_____

Strength

Proverbs 31:17-She sets about her work vigorously; her arms are strong for her tasks.

WALKING WITH A VIRTUOUS WOMAN

Prelude

We deal with so much daily, it's a surprise that some of us haven't completely lost our minds. Thank God for grace! The virtuous woman can handle what's in front of her. She handles it not because of herself; but because of the God that lives on the inside of her. It's important that as we go through life, we don't hold on to the superwoman mentality. That mentality causes you to think that you must handle it all on your own. God supplies grace to his children; grace to handle every single task. You don't need to pull on your own strength; doing so only leads to fatigue. You must pull on the strength of God. God's strength never runs out, never gets exhausted, and is never out of reach. You don't have to be superwoman. Take off the cape. His strength is available.

Prayer Day Five:

God, I first want to thank you for every time that you were my strength. I've had moments when I felt weak and didn't have the strength to move forward. You reminded me in your word, that your grace is sufficient for me; and your strength is made perfect in my times of weakness. God, thank you for grace. Thank you for releasing your grace to me, so that I can keep pressing forward on my hardest days. Father, I have tasks before me that require strength I don't have unless I have you! God, my heart's desire is to be a woman of great strength. I can't be strong without you. Father bless me with strength for the work that has been placed before me, and every task with my name on it. I need your strength to hold me up when I'm too exhausted to keep going. Bless me with supernatural strength during my moments of weakness. When I feel fatigued, drained, uninspired; when I lack motivation and drive, please be the good father that you are. Step in and hold up my arms. Lord, I know that I am weak without you. Be my strength as I face things in this life that have been designed to destroy me.

Declaration:

I declare I will walk in the strength of God, as I complete every task with my name on it.

Journal Prompt

What work is before you? What's the hardest thing about it?
What do you need God to do to help you through it?

_____

_____

_____

_____

_____

_____

_____

_____

_____

_____

_____

_____

_____

_____

_____

_____

_____

_____

_____

Vision

Proverbs 31:18-She sees that her trading is profitable, and her lamp does not go out at night.

Prelude

The virtuous woman has clear vision! She can see what she's carrying. She can see the value that she holds, as well as what she brings to the table. What's the vision for your life? You need to know where you're headed. Having vision is important because it allows you to get rid of everything that is not profitable to where you are going in life. There are so many areas in our lives that God wants to move in; but he won't until you get rid of what's not profitable. Having a clear understanding of God's vision for your life, allows you to decide what you will and will not be a part of, who you will and will not connect yourself to. Operate your life with your vision in mind. Ask yourself, "Will this choice be an asset or hindrance to the vision?" Vision is vital for the virtuous woman. You make poor choices and damaging decisions without proper vision. Understand that every step you take, every choice you make, affects the vision and everyone attached to it.

Prayer Day Six

Father open my eyes! Bless me with vision for my life. Let the vision burn within me to the point that I pursue it with no excuses. Your word declares to write the vision and make it plain upon tables, that he may run that readeth it. Open my eyes to understand what it is that you need for me to accomplish in this season. Reveal to me, Lord, the areas of my life that need improvement in order to make it to the next level. Show me what you need for me to learn in this season. Clear my eyes to see the purpose that you have for my life. God, grant me vision for my family, and vision for the affairs that you have put me over. Let me not grow weary in well doing, as your word declares in due season I will reap if I faint not. Let me stand tall and firm in the position that you place me in. Lord don't allow my vision to die. Anything in my life that may be hindering me from seeing clearly, Father, I pray in the name of Jesus that you remove it. Every hindrance, every stumbling block, be removed in the name of Jesus. Father allow me to look and see what is profitable. Remove everything from my life that serves no purpose for the vision that you gave me.

Declaration:

I declare my vision be open, and everything in my life that is not profitable for the vision be removed.

Journal Prompt

What is not profitable to your vision?
How can you remove it?
What are you doing to work towards the vision that God has given
you?

_____

_____

_____

_____

_____

_____

_____

_____

_____

_____

_____

_____

_____

_____

_____

_____

_____

_____

Assignment

Proverbs 31:19-In her hand she holds the distaff and grasps the spindle with her fingers.

WALKING WITH A VIRTUOUS WOMAN

Prelude

What was the last thing God told you to do? Did you complete it? There are a lot of assignments that you have tucked away in a folder and placed in the back of the closet. It's time for you to pull those things out and get them done! Your decision not to fulfill your assignment has an impact on the earth. As we look at our individual assignment, understand that it goes beyond you. Completing it will have an impact on someone else's life. Whose life hasn't experienced godly impact because you stuck your assignment under your bed? God has everyone here for a reason; to fulfill a purpose...what's yours?

Prayer Day Seven

Lord, there are so many things that the world presents to me. The world tells me their version of success; but God, I want to be successful in your eyes. Lord don't allow me to get caught up in the world's definition of success. Allow me Lord, to focus completely on the assignment that you have placed before me. Father show me what you've assigned me to do. God, I know that everything you created, you created on purpose, for a purpose. Lord, I need you to show me why you created me. Lord, reveal to me where you want my hands working. Father teach me the importance of completing the assignment that you've placed before me. Lord, I pray that my assignment will bless generations to come. Bless me Father with the strength and grace to carry out my assignment. Sometimes it seems too hard to accomplish. Sometimes I don't think that I'm skilled enough to accomplish it. Sometimes I don't feel that I'm equipped enough to handle it. This discourages me and makes me want to turn from the assignment. Father remind me during those, moments that you would've never given me the assignment, if you didn't think that I was capable of handling it. Father give me the momentum to keep going. When I feel tired, remind me that my assignment isn't just about me. Lord, I never want to be caught without the distaff in my hand and grasping the spindle. I want you to always find me on assignment. Lord grant me favor that this assignment may produce fruit in the lives of your people.

Declaration:

I declare successful completion of the assignment that God has given me.

Journal Prompt

What is the hardest thing about your assignment?Are you giving it
your all? Why or why not?

_____

_____

_____

_____

_____

_____

_____

_____

_____

_____

_____

_____

_____

_____

_____

_____

_____

_____

Giving

Proverbs 31:20- She opens her arms to the poor and extends her hands to the needy.

Prelude

There are people all over the world right now that are standing in need! We have the honor of being God's hands and feet here on the earth, to assist people in their time of need. I know it's easy to keep your money in your pocket and stay to yourself. As a woman of God, we must open our arms to those that are in need. God didn't bless us to keep it to ourselves. He gives seed to the sower (2 Corinthians 9:10 King James Version). He gives to those that are willing to give. I challenge you to give as God allows you to, with a cheerful heart. Don't get stuck in the mindset of only giving to those that look like you or come from the same city as you. Reach out to those that are in need; no matter race, gender, ethnicity, or social class... just give.

Prayer Day Eight

God, I thank you that giving is who you are. You are a God that gives with no second thought. You have been giving since the beginning of time; and you haven't stopped yet. Lord, I thank you for giving the gift that no one can beat; the gift of your son Jesus Christ. I'm thankful Lord, that none of your children walk in lack, because you are a good Father that takes care of his children. Just as David said, "I have never seen the righteous forsaken, nor its seed begging for bread," you always find a way to supply my needs and you give selflessly. Lord, teach me how to be that kind of giver. Teach me Lord, to give of my time, wisdom, money, love, and kind words, towards those that stand in need. I want to receive people with open arms. I want them to experience your love when they meet me. Let me not ignore a person that's standing in need. If I don't have what they need, show me the direction to point them in to get the help that they are asking for. Father, this world stands in need; as I am your hands and feet here in the earth. Use me to help those that are living in lack. Let me give with wisdom and by the leading of Holy Spirit. Bless me Father, with arms that open and hands that extend to those in need. Your word declares that you give seed to the sower. Bless me so that I may be able to give. Lord, I want to be able to give cheerfully and not grudgingly. Your word declares that you love a cheerful giver. Lord, I desire for you to love the giver that I am. Father teach me to give from my heart; not for recognition, not for social media acknowledgement, not for a pat on the back; but because my heart desires to give. Lord be pleased with my giving.

Declaration:

I declare seed will be placed in my hands to give.

Journal Prompt

What could you give more of? When was the last time you helped
someone in need? How did it make you feel?

_____

_____

_____

_____

_____

_____

_____

_____

_____

_____

_____

_____

_____

_____

_____

_____

_____

_____

_____

Fearless

Proverbs 31:21-When it snows, she has no fear for her household; for all of them are clothed in scarlet.

WALKING WITH A VIRTUOUS WOMAN

Prelude

At one time or another, most of us have faced fear head-on. Fear of the dark, the boogieman, heights, spiders, and the future. The list is endless. As a woman of virtue, it is your responsibility to make sure you never allow fear to control you. A mind set of fear always prevents us from living our life to its fullest potential. It causes us to be in a perpetual state of anxiety and panic. God does not want his daughters to live their lives trembling because they are afraid of what will or won't happen next. The virtuous woman is fearless! She knows that God will take care of her, her family, and everything that is of concern to her. One of the amazing things about belonging to God, is that he cares about what's concerning you. Woman of God, what are you concerned about? What are you afraid of? Have you voiced those fears and concerns to God? God wants to know what's going on in your household. Your fears are his fights; and he has never lost a battle!

Prayer Day Nine

Lord, fear is such a liar! It cripples your people, and sometimes it holds me back from doing what you called me to do. Father, I want to be a fearless servant. I do have times when I am afraid. I no longer want to operate like that. I no longer want fear to be a part of my life. Father, your word declares that you have not given me the spirit of fear but of power, love, and a sound mind. I declare that fear has no place in my life. You said, "fear not for I am with you." God, during the times that fear shows its ugly face, remind me that you are with me. I have no reason to fear when I have the Great, I am, in my corner. No matter what discouraging news shows up at my door, I declare that I will not fear. I will not run in fear when things begin to fall apart. I will instead run to the throne and trust that you will get me through everything that I face. God, thank you for giving me the authority to live a fearless life.

Declaration:

I declare that fear has no place in my life.

Journal Prompt

What is your biggest fear?
What can you do to overcome it?

_____

_____

_____

_____

_____

_____

_____

_____

_____

_____

_____

_____

_____

_____

_____

_____

_____

_____

_____

Modest

Proverbs 31:22- She makes coverings for her bed; she is clothed in fine linen and purple.

Prelude

What a woman wears says a lot about her and speaks loudly of the way that she sees herself. It is important as a woman of virtue that you honor God and yourself with the way you dress. I know you're probably thinking, "Whitney, I'm of age. I wear what I want to wear." You are correct! My challenge to you is to be more conscious of what you put on, and the message that your clothes send to those that see you. You want to be viewed as a woman of dignity, respect, and honor. 'If you got it, flaunt it,' has been a motto created by society, and written on the hearts of so many women. As a woman of virtue, you can't abide by cultural principles and what they view as normal. We are not sex symbols. We are not to be objectified or flaunt our bodies to show that we're "grown." Class and grace must always be our garments.

Prayer Day Ten

Lord, there are so many examples around me encouraging me to be ok with exposing my body to the world. Father allow me to set a new standard. Allow me to inspire women to be modest. Let me adorn myself in a modest way, recognizing that my body is to be cherished. Lord, let your holy Spirit convict me in the times when I attempt to dress myself in a way that is acceptable to the world; but dishonorable to you and my body. Teach me to be a woman with class and elegance. I want to be adorned in fine linen and purple. Let what I wear represent you well. Teach me Lord, the importance of self-worth and to value my body because I am your daughter, your vessel. I don't want to wear things that entice your sons and cause them to lust. Allow me Lord, to be an inspiration to other women to dress in a modest manner. I want to carry myself like a woman of God should. I want to represent you with my garments.

Declaration:

I declare that I am valuable, and I will dress in a manner that is honorable to God and my body.

Journal Prompt
How can you make modesty popular?

_____

_____

_____

_____

_____

_____

_____

_____

_____

_____

_____

_____

_____

_____

_____

_____

_____

An Honorable Mate

Proverbs 31:23-Her husband is respected at the city gate, where he takes his seat among the elders of the land.

WALKING WITH A VIRTUOUS WOMAN

Prelude

Who we choose to get into covenant with must be handled with caution and prayer! Attaching yourself to someone based on superficial values like how he looks, where he works, what he drives, is not the way we are to choose a mate. The first question to ask is, "Is he suitable?" Suitability is far more important than compatibility. You can meet someone who is compatible, but not suitable. You both can share the same interest, and he not be a fit for what God is doing in your life. A suitable person fits you, your purpose, your assignment, and where God is taking you. For him to be suitable, he must be a man that honors God! If he doesn't honor God, it's going to be hard for him to love you, as Christ loved the church. As a woman of virtue, a man of respect is a fit for you.

Prayer Day Eleven

Father I thank you for relationship and divine connection. I thank you for crafting life in a way, that you connect and disconnect us from people, from season to season. Father, in this moment I pray for my mate. I pray Lord, that he is honored by many. Let him be honored not because of a bad reputation or irate behavior. Let him be respected because he belongs to you. I pray that doors are opened for him. I pray that his gift puts him before great men. Let people both near and far, respect him and honor him because of his walk with you. Touch him Father, so that he is a man of integrity and respect. Let your word be his moral compass and your spirit be his guide. Touch his mind and bless him with wisdom God. Allow him to handle every situation that he faces with your instruction. Let his flesh not get the best of him. Father, I desire him to be an honorable man. Be his help so that he can be a provider for his family. Allow him to lead his household with truth and compassion.

Declaration:

I declare that my mate will be a man of integrity, and he will be honored by people both near and far.

64

Journal Prompt

What can you do to be a great help to your mate?
What are things that you can say to encourage him?

_____

_____

_____

_____

_____

_____

_____

_____

_____

_____

_____

_____

_____

_____

_____

_____

_____

_____

_____

Resourceful

Proverbs 31:24-She makes linen garments and sells them and supplies the merchants with sashes.

Prelude

One of the many things I learned from my mother while in the kitchen is use what you got. There were times when I opened the refrigerator with immature eyes and concluded there was nothing to eat. My mother would enter the same kitchen, and whip together an entire meal using the principle use what you got. She taught me the importance of being resourceful. Are you using what you got? Are you fully utilizing the resources that are available to you? I truly believe that God will send you what you need; but it's up to you to pay attention to what he has sent. Often, we overlook the resource because it wasn't sent in the way we expected. There are things laying around us that we have not looked at, to see how it could be of use to us. A virtuous woman takes what she has, uses it to advance the kingdom of God, and bring profit to her home. for you.

Prayer Day Twelve

God, I thank you for the things that I didn't even know were blessings when you initially gave them to me. Lord, I know that I'm not worthy or deserving of any of it. There isn't enough time in the day to thank you for all the things that you've blessed me with. You are such a good Father. Lord, I ask that you show me how to take what you've given me to bring revenue to my home. Lord, teach me how to be resourceful. Teach me Lord, how to utilize what you've given me, to provide for my family and to be an asset to the household. God, bless me with the ability to create! Lord, I pray for inventions, business plans, and multiple streams of income, in the name of Jesus. Father grant me the ability to see and create. Touch my mind Lord, so that I recognize what's in front of me and how to use it. Let nothing that I have go to waste. Father, I pour myself out to you; fill me up with your spirit, Lord. Let your spirit work through me as I operate business. Make me a great businesswoman; a woman operating business with the love of God, truth, and integrity. Let me set an example amongst believers and non-believers, on how to operate business in God's way.

Declaration:

I declare everything in me and around me will be utilized to advance the kingdom of God. I declare multiple streams of income.

Journal Prompt

Are you utilizing everything you must to be an asset to the home
and the kingdom of God? Why or why not?

_____

_____

_____

_____

_____

_____

_____

_____

_____

_____

_____

_____

_____

_____

_____

_____

_____

_____

_____

Joyful

Proverbs 31:25-She is clothed with strength and dignity; she can laugh at the days to come.

WALKING WITH A VIRTUOUS WOMAN

Prelude

The virtuous woman maintains her joy. Not because everything in her life is going right; but because she knows who she serves! Don't find yourself putting your joy in the hands of people, money, opportunities, jobs, or material things. The problem with that is, when those things leave, they take your joy with them. When my joy is in God, and comes from God, it's something that cannot be taken away from me. Woman of God, you maintain your joy not by everything being in order, or all your ducks in a row; your joy is sustained because you know who the source of that joy is! It's easy to have joy when things are going right; but can you have that same joy when the bills are piling up, your family is falling apart, and nothing seems to be going right? Your joy should not be conditional. It doesn't come and go based upon your circumstances. Joy is a characteristic that you maintain regardless of what's going on around you. Joy during sorrow shows the enemy that no matter what he throws at you, your joy will not be shaken.

Prayer Day Thirteen

Lord, I've had so many hurtful things happen in my life, that smiling is now hard to do. I've lost things and people. I've been mistreated, rejected, abandoned; and these things have taken my smile. I often wonder is there a reason to smile? God, I don't want to be the woman that allows circumstances to choose whether I smile or not. I don't want to be the woman that allows loss to take her smile away. Teach me to smile no matter what. Teach me to maintain joy, no matter what. You said, "Count it all joy when you fall in diverse temptations." In the moments when I began to feel discouraged, remind me to keep smiling. I can keep smiling because I know that no matter what I lose, I will always have you. I have no need to fear or worry about tomorrow, because you are already there. I can smile and laugh at the days that are ahead of me, because I have the Great, I am, watching over me. Lord, I never want to find myself bitter, jealous, envious or prideful. I want to be full of joy! Let the joy that I have, reflect the confidence that I have in you. Lord you promised to give me a joy the world cannot give, and the world cannot take away. I know that I'll have some tough days; but Lord, remind me of your faithfulness, so that my smile can be restored.

Declaration:

I declare the joy of the Lord will be my strength. I will rejoice in the middle of all situations.

Journal Prompt

What tampers with your joy?
How can you prevent situations from stealing your joy?

_____

_____

_____

_____

_____

_____

_____

_____

_____

_____

_____

_____

_____

_____

_____

_____

_____

_____

_____

Godly Speech

Proverbs 31:26- She speaks with wisdom, and
faithful instruction is on her tongue.

WALKING WITH A VIRTUOUS WOMAN

Prelude

Unfortunately, women all over the world have been labeled as gossipers; but we have the ability to change that narrative! Woman of God be more conscious of the words that you speak. We are to make sure that our communication is seasoned with salt (Colossians 4:6 King James Version). The words that we speak should edify, encourage, and empower; if they aren't doing those things, then we need to check our speech. Hold yourself accountable for the things that you say, because your words are powerful. Life and death are in the power of the tongue; and as a woman of virtue, you want to be found speaking life. Not just speaking life regarding other people; but also, your own life. We must be more careful with what we speak about ourselves.

Prayer Day Fourteen

Father, forgive me for the times that I spoke in a way that wasn't pleasing to you. Forgive me for the times that I used my tongue to tear down my brother or sister. I'm sorry for the times that I spoke things that were ugly, hurtful, and untrue. I want to be the kind of woman that speaks with kindness and wisdom. Teach me how to speak with kindness. Your word declares that kind words are like honey; sweet to the soul and healthy for the body. Let kind words flow from my tongue naturally. I want to be able to speak well of people, to speak life into people. Bless me with wisdom beyond my years. When people have conversations with me, let them recognize that I have been with God. Let me not speak from my flesh. Allow my speech to be fruitful and uplifting. I don't want to be found gossiping or slandering another person's name. I want to be found calling their name out in prayer. Let people have conversation with me, and recognize that I'm different because of my speech. Allow my speech to be Godly.

Declaration:

I declare my words will be medicine. I declare my speech will be full of wisdom and kindness.

Journal Prompt

Who around you needs to have life spoken into them?
How have you made sure kind words are spoken into their life?
What godly speech can you speak over your life?

_____

_____

_____

_____

_____

_____

_____

_____

_____

_____

_____

_____

_____

_____

_____

_____

_____

_____

_____

_____

_____

Watchful

Proverbs 31:27- She watches over the affairs of her household and does not eat the bread of idleness.

WALKING WITH A VIRTUOUS WOMAN

Prelude

My mother often said, "A woman's home is a reflection of her." What is

your home saying about you? How are you doing with the upkeep and

maintenance of it? Not just the physical upkeep, but the spiritual upkeep

as well. We understand the importance of the physical upkeep of our

home; cleaning, maintaining our bills, repairs. But spiritual maintenance

is even more important. The virtuous woman maintains the spiritual

upkeep of her home. She keeps her household covered in prayer. She is

cautious with what she allows in and out, maintains peace, love, and unity,

in the four walls of her home. Woman of God, you must always keep your

eyes open! Be sober-minded and fully aware of what's going on in your

household. The affairs of your household are your responsibility; handle

them with care. As God gives us things, it is our responsibility to take care

of them; so be deliberate about taking care of home first!

Prayer Day Fifteen

Father, life has a way of distracting me. The enemy always finds a way to send distractions, and before I know it, the wrong thing has my attention and focus. I no longer want to operate like that. Lord give me focus! Give me doves eyes; eyes that are solely focused on you, and what you have assigned me to do. Lord, let my focus be on the affairs of my home. I want to be watchful over what you've put in my care. I want to be found taking care of what you've blessed me with. Let me not partake of the bread of idleness. I want to be found being about my Father's business. I have no time to waste. You said in your word, "Work while it is day for the night cometh when no man can work." Teach me Lord, the importance of being focused and watchful over what you've blessed me with. You said to be sober and vigilant because Satan is like a roaring lion, seeking whom he may devour. I refuse to be the enemy's prey; he will not devour me. He will not catch me sleeping on the job, sleeping on my purpose, assignment, goals, or relationship with you. I will be watchful. Father. I thank you for everything that you've entrusted me with. To show my appreciation, I will take good care of it. I will watch over it. The way the shepherd watches over his sheep. I want to take care of the affairs of my home, making sure things are together and in order. I will no longer waste the valuable time that you've given me, on things that distract me. It's time to get focused on things that matter. Lord teach me to be watchful. Teach me to fix my eyes on the things that are important.

Declaration:

I declare that I will not be the enemy's prey, I will be sober and vigilant.

Journal Prompt

What are your distractions?
What are things you can do to turn from them?

_____

_____

_____

_____

_____

_____

_____

_____

_____

_____

_____

_____

_____

_____

_____

_____

_____

_____

_____

_____

Familial Impact

Proverbs 31:28- Her children arise and call her blessed; her husband also, and he praises her.

WALKING WITH A VIRTUOUS WOMAN

Prelude

Every step, every choice, every desire you attempt to obtain, will not just impact you, but those connected to you as well! I know we get in the habit of saying, "This is my life." This is your life; but your life has impact on the lives of other people. This is a big charge to carry; but it's also an honor. As you say yes to God, not only will you benefit from it, but others will as well. Our yes to God isn't just about us. We have people attached to us; generations attached to us that will be affected because of our obedience to God. Knowing that what you do in your life can cause someone to pursue God, is an honor.

Prayer Day Sixteen

Father grace me to impact my family. Allow them to see the life I live and have a desire to live for you. Lord I want my walk with you, and the life that I live for you, to not only inspire strangers; but those in my family as well. I want those in my home to have a desire to serve you, because of how well I speak about you. Lord allow the life that I live to affect generations. Let my children, and my grandchildren, walk in abundance because of the 'yes' that I've given to you. Let the blessings not just stop and end with me. Allow my family to look at me and all the things that I've overcome and be inspired to never give up. Lord, I desire for my entire family to be saved. I desire for my household to be saved. I want to impact my family. I want my purpose to have so much impact, that people I'll never even meet, accept Jesus Christ as their savior. Lord don't let my impact in this world die when I take my last breath. Allow my legacy to be produced through my walk with you.

Declaration:

I declare that my walk will bless generations, and my yes to God will impact family.

Journal Prompt

What have you done to inspire your family to live for God?

_____

_____

_____

_____

_____

_____

_____

_____

_____

_____

_____

_____

_____

_____

_____

_____

_____

_____

_____

Godly Example

Proverbs 31:29- Many women do noble things, but you surpass them all.

WALKING WITH A VIRTUOUS WOMAN

Prelude

Entertainment offers so many examples on what a woman should look like, act like, talk like, and walk like. We are bombarded with images all day. Although there is nothing wrong with some of the things being presented to us, we must filter them through the word of God. As a woman of virtue, our code of conduct comes from scripture. The virtuous woman understands that scripture is her reference on how she is to carry herself. Keeping the word of God written over our hearts, allows us to obey it and be an example of it. There are women all over the world, in search of someone that they can look up to. Woman of God, you should be that woman. Women should be able to look at you, and be inspired to pursue God, to never give up, and to walk in her God-given authority. What example are you setting? What can the people around you say that they've learned from the life you've lived before them? What model are you presenting to them? It's important to make sure that the example you are setting is laced with the word of God and led by the Holy Spirit.

Prayer Day Seventeen:

Lord there are so many examples of what a woman should be that are presented to me daily. Examples are shoved in my face on tv, in magazines, on social media, and in my day to day life. I'm often bombarded with the idea of what a woman should be according to the world's standards. God, I want to exemplify the standard that you have set. I want to reflect your word. The world has an idea of what a woman should be; but you know what you designed woman to be. I want to be a woman that maintains her morals and standards. I want to be a Godly example for other women. Father teach me how to carry myself like a Godly woman. Let nothing I do look like the world. Let women look at me and notice that I'm different than the rest. Let that difference inspire them to carry themselves with class and grace. I just want to represent you well, Father. I can't do this in my own strength. I need you. Hold me up with your righteous right hand; and remind me to maintain the standard when I feel like fitting in. Allow my life to be an example for other women.

Declaration:

I declare that I will carry myself as a woman of God. I will not fit in with the world. I will be a woman with morals, standards, and substance.

Journal Prompt

What women around you, can you inspire?
How can you inspire them?

_____

_____

_____

_____

_____

_____

_____

_____

_____

_____

_____

_____

_____

_____

_____

_____

_____

_____

God Fearing

Proverbs 31:30- Charm is deceptive, and beauty is fleeting; but a woman who fears the LORD is to be praised.

WALKING WITH A VIRTUOUS WOMAN

Prelude

To be God-fearing means to have such a reverence and respect for God, that it impacts the way we live our lives. Does the way you live your life say that you revere God? You should want to be known as the woman who respects God! It's ok to be known as the best dressed, attractive, and educated; but those things will pass away. The way you live for God will outlive you! Years from now, decades from now, people will speak on the type of God-fearing woman you were. You want to establish a reputation that is built on God, and always includes God. Honor him with every area of your life; even the areas that no one sees. Honor him in your private moments, inboxes, text messages. Even when the doors are closed, honor God.

Prayer Day Eighteen:

Lord, I never want to be found disrespecting you. I want to respect you in speech, conduct, and thoughts. I want to be found always reverencing and honoring you. I want to make sure that with everything I do, you get the glory out of it. I want you to look at me and be pleased. I know that there will be times when I will fall. Your word declares that a righteous man falleth seven times. Teach me not to get comfortable with the fall. Let people respect me because of the relationship that I have with you. You said in your word that when a man pleases God, even his enemies are at peace with him. Let those that dislike me, still be at peace with me because they know that I serve you. There's nothing wrong with being beautiful; but I never want people to get caught up in my outer shell. Lord, let me not get caught up in my looks either. Teach me to be more concerned with my inner-beauty than my outer-beauty. I want the inner woman to be pleasing in your sight. You said that it is the unfading beauty of a gentle and quiet spirit that is of great worth in your sight. I have a desire to honor you and be pleasing to you. I want to live a life that honors you; especially in those moments when no one is around. Father, I want my private life to please you, as well as my public life. I want every area of my life to be pleasing to you.

Declaration:

I declare that I will be God-fearing. Every area of my life will be pleasing to my Father.

Journal Prompt

What areas in your life are displeasing to God?
What can you do to ensure those areas are fixed?

_____

_____

_____

_____

_____

_____

_____

_____

_____

_____

_____

_____

_____

_____

_____

_____

_____

_____

Being a Light

Proverbs 31:31-Honor her for all that
her hands have done, and let her works
bring her praise at the city gate.

WALKING WITH A VIRTUOUS WOMAN

Prelude

You ever been in darkness and blindly searched for just a small beacon of light? That's how we are in places of darkness. We are that small beacon of light. As we work for God and pursue him wholeheartedly, people are watching us. They watch the way we handle tough situations. They watch us both in unfavorable moments, and times of frustrations. These times give us the opportunity to show them who we serve! As you serve God, it will inspire others to serve Him in that moment; you're being a light. It's easy to fade into the darkness; but as the light, you always have to be illuminated. There is someone at the point where they want to give up; and you, the light, show up as a beacon of hope! Your light is powerful and it's lifesaving. Always keep it on.

Prayer Day Nineteen

Lord, thank you for being the light of my life. Before you, I couldn't see where I was going. I was lost. I had no sense of purpose or direction. When you came in, everything began to change for the better. Your presence in my life has been life-changing! You have made me a better woman. I still have things that I need to work on; but I'm not the same woman I used to be. As I work towards becoming a better woman, let my work inspire others to work. Let my light be seen; not for me, but for you. Just as you said, "Let your light shine before others, that they may see your good deeds and glorify your Father in heaven." Lord, let my light lead people to you. If there's anything in my life that's dimming my light, remove it from my life. I know that the enemy is going to present things to me that have been created to dim my light. Lord, give me self-control to resist it. You said if I resist the devil he will flee. Teach me the importance of resisting the enemy. My light is too important, and too powerful, to be dimmed by some temporary stuff the enemy has offered me. Allow my light to shine in the moments that it's needed most.

Declaration:

I declare that I will be a light in this dark world. People will recognize my works and know that I belong to God.

Journal Prompt

Where does your light shine the most?
Where does your light shine the least and why?

_____

_____

_____

_____

_____

_____

_____

_____

_____

_____

_____

_____

_____

_____

_____

_____

_____

_____

Worth

Proverbs 31:10-A wife of noble charcter who can find? She is worth far more than rubies.

Prelude

The world has tried to convince us that our worth is found in our relationship status, our bank account, our accomplishments, and our looks. The virtuous woman does not base her worth or her value on the things that she has acquired. She is worthy because God says she is worthy. She is valuable because God calls her valuable. The moment you begin to realize how valuable you are in the eyes of God, it makes you approach life differently. What you don't want to do is base your worth on a bunch of tangible things. The danger in that is when those things fade away, your worth goes right along with it. God's definition of worthiness is not based on tangible things. He valued you so much that he was willing to send his son to the cross to die for you. Just because you don't have the degrees, the money, the homes, the cars, the popularity, does not take anything away from your worth. Those things are simply accessories; apart from them you are still worthy. The benefit of knowing your worth is that it causes you to make better decisions. The decisions that you make are based upon the way that you view yourself. When you understand that your price is far above rubies, you don't settle, compromise, or demean yourself. You walk with integrity and confidence. Don't allow this world to convince you that worth is based on stuff, because it's not. God already calls you worthy; it's time for you to live like it!

Prayer Day Twenty:

God, I am so grateful that you call me worthy. Not because I've accomplished amazing things; not because of my gifts, my level of education, but because I'm your daughter! It is such an honor that I'm able to call you Father, and that you call me worthy. This world can sometimes make me feel like I'm not good enough. When those thoughts arise, remind me of your word that declares I am worthy. I'm not perfect. I've made mistakes and will probably make more; but you promised if I confess my sins to you that you are faithful and just to forgive. I'm grateful for everything that you've blessed me with; but don't allow me to base my worth on those things. Correct me in the moments when I determine my value based on the things that I have accumulated. God, I need to be reminded daily that I am worthy because you have spoken it over me. I know that the enemy will try to convince me that I have no value, but I will boldly declare that in the eyes of God I am worthy!

Declaration:

God calls me worthy; therefore, I AM WORTHY.

Journal Prompt

How would you define worth? Think of a time when your
confidence was challenged. How did you respond?

_____

_____

_____

_____

_____

_____

_____

_____

_____

_____

_____

_____

_____

_____

_____

_____

_____

_____

_____

_____

Trustworthy

Proverbs 31:11
Her husband can trust her,
and she will greatly enrich his life.

WALKING WITH A VIRTUOUS WOMAN

Prelude

A woman of virtue can be trusted! The heart of her husband safely

trusts in her. Those are #wifegoals. To know that someone can

safely trust in you is such a great quality to have. Can people trust

you? Can they tell you sensitive information and not worry about

you sharing it? When you tell them something, can they trust your

words? If you tell them you're going to be there, can they trust that

you'll show up? Trust is a trait that every woman of virtue should

carry in her back pocket. Culture encourages us to trust no one; as

a woman of God, you have been positioned to change the way that

people view trust. There will come moments when trust will be put

to the test. That's the only way to show that you have it. Evidence

of trust is only shown when it's needed. Not only is trust needed

in your relationship with people, but also with God. Can God trust

you? Can he reveal things to you and not worry about you

mismanaging that revelation? Can he give you the desires of your

heart, and trust you not to mishandle them? There are things that

have not been released. It's not because God doesn't want us to

have them; but because we can't be trusted with them. One of the

amazing things about God is that he knows our heart. He is fully

aware of our hearts and he knows if trust isn't present there.

Prayer Day Twenty One

God thank you for being the epitome of trustworthiness. I can't recall a time when I couldn't trust you. Thank you for every moment where I had to rely on trusting you. Thank you for the times that were uncomfortable but taught me to trust you. I pray that you would help me become a woman of trust. Not only do I want my husband, children, friends, and family to trust me; but God, I want to be trusted by you. I don't want to miss out on what you have for me; nor do I want to displease you due to a lack of trust. Teach me to trust you more and teach me how to become a woman that can be trusted.

Declaration:

I can be trusted by man. I can be trusted by God.

Journal Prompt

Would you consider yourself trustworthy?
Why or why not?Name a time when your trust was tested.
